24

The SECRET LIVES of Animals

The Secret Lives of

Wolves

by Julia Barnes

GARETH STEVENS
GS PUBLISHING
A Member of the WRC Media Family of Companies

Please visit our web site at: www.garethstevens.com
For a free color catalog describing Gareth Stevens Publishing's list of high-quality books
and multimedia programs, call 1-800-542-2595 (USA) or 1-800-387-3178 (Canada).
Gareth Stevens Publishing's fax: (414) 332-3567.

Library of Congress Cataloging-in-Publication Data

Barnes, Julia, 1955–
    The secret lives of wolves / Julia Barnes.
       p. cm. — (The secret lives of animals)
    Includes bibliographical references and index.
    ISBN–13: 978-0-8368-7660-4 (lib. bdg.)
    1. Wolves—Juvenile literature.   I. Title.
    QL737.C22B3395   2007
    599.773—dc22   2006035331

This North American edition first published in 2007 by
Gareth Stevens Publishing
A Member of the WRC Media Family of Companies
330 West Olive Street, Suite 100
Milwaukee, WI 53212 USA

This edition copyright © 2007 by Gareth Stevens Inc.
Original edition copyright © 2006 by Westline Publishing.
Additional end matter copyright 2007 by Gareth Stevens, Inc.

Gareth Stevens editor: Gini Holland
Gareth Stevens designer: Kami M. Strunsee
Gareth Stevens art direction: Tammy West
Gareth Stevens Library production: Jessica Yanke and Robert Kraus

Photo credits: © istockphoto.com: Lukasz Chyrek front cover, p. 19; Chris Crafter p. 14;
Len Tillim p. 17; Holly Kucher p. 20; Olga Mirenska p. 21; Christopher O Driscoll p. 23;
Denis Pepin p. 27; © Oxford Scientici Films: Alan and Sandy Carey p. 24. All other images
copyright © Westline Ltd.

Printed in the United States of America

1 2 3 4 5 6 7 8 9 10 10 09 08 07 06

Contents

Introducing the Wolf

The wolf is one of the great team players of the animal world. It lives in a pack, and its survival depends on living with, and cooperating with, other pack members. The wolf is an animal that forms very close ties with other wolves and obeys the rule of the **pack leader**. What is life really like for the wolf? How does a wolf spend its days? What are its favorite pastimes? How does it communicate with other wolves?

To find out all about wolves, we need to enter their secret world.

SECRETS OF SUCCESS

The wolf is a very **adaptable** animal and can make its home in lots of different places. Wolves live in forests, open plains, deserts, and mountains. They have spread around the world and were once the most widespread **mammal** on land in the animal kingdom. Now, however, they are endangered.

The wolf is a tough animal that can endure harsh living conditions.

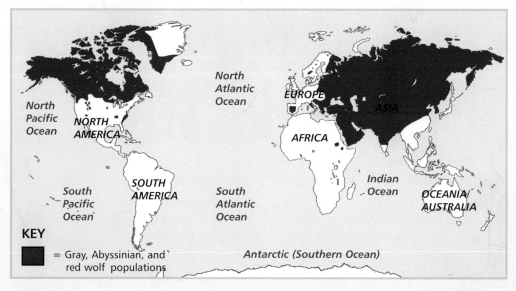

KEY

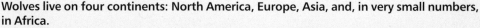
= Gray, Abyssinian, and red wolf populations

Wolves live on four continents: North America, Europe, Asia, and, in very small numbers, in Africa.

What has made the wolf such a great survivor?

- The wolf hunts in packs, so it is able to bring down huge **prey animals** that provide large amounts of food.
- An animal that lives in a pack is hard to attack, so the wolf has few natural enemies.
- Only the top male and female in a pack produce a litter, which gives the cubs the best chance of surviving.
- Wolves can live in extreme temperatures of heat and cold.

WHERE DO WOLVES LIVE?

The gray wolf, also known as the the timber wolf, is found in North America, Europe, Asia, and the Middle East. The biggest gray wolf populations live in Russia, where there are 40,000 to 60,000 wolves. Canada has about 40,000 wolves, and Alaska has 6,000. There are about 2,700 wolves living in the lower forty-eight states of the United States.

Two other kinds of wolves, the red wolf and the Abyssinian wolf, are close to extinct. The red wolf has recently been reintroduced into wild life preserves in the United States, where it is being helped to survive. The Abyssinian wolf lives in Ethiopia, Africa, and is critically endangered, with only about five hundred to seven hundred left.

Understanding the Ways of the Wolf

The wolf has found a home in many different places and can survive in harsh living conditions. It has been able to adapt to many environments, from frozen arctic regions to hot deserts. Like all animals, however, a wolf needs a few essential things to survive.

FINDING A HOME

Usually about six adults, plus a number of cubs, make up a wolf pack. So that all members get enough to eat, the pack must have its own home **territory** where it can hunt without competition from other wolf packs. The size

A wolf pack is a tight-knit family group that lives and hunts together.

6

of a pack's territory will depend on the availability of prey. If a large number of hoofed animals, which are the wolf's preferred prey, are abundant, the territory may be only 25 square miles (65 square kilometers). Where fewer animals exist, the wolf's territory may need to be as large as 1,000 square miles (2,600 sq km).

FOOD

The wolf is successful in the wild because it hunts in a pack and can bring down an animal that is much larger than itself. A wolf pack will tackle an animal as big as a bison, which may weigh nearly a ton (0.9 tonne) and is ten times larger than a single wolf! Wolves hunt deer, elk, caribou, pronghorn, musk oxes, mountain goats, and mountain sheep. If large prey animals are in short supply, wolves make do with beavers, hares, rabbits, rodents, and even berries when they are in season.

A PACK

A wolf has a better chance of surviving if it belongs to a pack.

A lone wolf cannot hunt large animals and may be attacked by other meat-eating hunters. A wolf pack is divided between males and females. The females obey the **top-ranking** female; the males obey the top-ranking male. The pack leader may be a male or a female. The leader's job is to keep peace in the pack and to make all the important decisions, such as when to hunt and when to go traveling.

All members of the pack obey the rule of the pack leader, which can be either male or female.

7

The Wolf's Perfect Body

The wolf is a lean, rugged-looking animal, but it has the perfect body for tracking prey over long distances and then going in for the kill.

SIZE AND BUILD

An adult wolf stands between 26 to 28 inches (66 to 71 centimeters) tall at the shoulder and is more than 6 feet (1.8 meters) long from its nose to the end of its tail. That is twice the size of a German shepherd dog. Males are always bigger than females and weigh between 60 and 100 pounds (27 to 45 kilograms).

A wolf can run at 43.5 miles (70 kilometers) per hour, but it can only keep this up for short distances. The wolf is built for **endurance**. A wolf pack may travel more than 20 miles (32 km) in one day and will keep on the move for days at a time. The wolf travels at a steady trot, traveling at about 7.5 to 10 miles (12 to 16 km) per hour.

The wolf is lean and agile and will travel at a steady trot over rough ground, crossing water when necessary.

TEETH

The wolf's teeth are designed to bite its prey and then to eat the **carcass**. The largest teeth are the four **canines,** or fangs, which are in the upper and lower jaws. These are used for biting into the prey animal and holding onto it. The canines may measure 2.25 inches (5.7 cm) in length. The wolf does not chew. Instead, it slices meat with its teeth and swallows it in small chunks. The wolf also has very powerful jaws, which are used to crush bones and get at the **marrow** that is inside. In this way, very little of a kill goes to waste.

The wolf's thick winter coat keeps it warm even in the very coldest weather.

COAT

The wolf has a fur coat for all seasons of the year, so it can survive extremes of heat and cold. A Mexican wolf that lives in the Arizona desert puts up with freezing cold winters of minus 60 °Fahrenheit (-51 °Celsius) and boiling hot summers where the temperature may reach 115 °F (46 °C). These numbers make a difference of 175 degrees Fahrenheit (97 degrees Celsius), which is a huge temperature range. To survive this range, the wolf has a double coat, which consists of a topcoat and a thick, woolly undercoat. A wolf starts to grow a thick coat in the fall. When warmer weather comes in the spring, the wolf gradually sheds its undercoat.

Wolves come in many different shades of gray. Some appear almost cream, while others are nearly black. The coat colors act as **camouflage**, so the wolf can blend in with its surroundings and appear invisible when it is hunting.

How a Wolf Sees the World

Imagine yourself inside the furry, four-legged body of a wolf to find out how the world appears if you are a meat-eating **predator** with great hearing and a keen sense of smell.

EYESIGHT

The wolf can see as well as we do, but it relies far more on its hearing and sense of smell when hunting. The wolf's eyes are placed at the front of its head, so it looks directly in front and to the sides. The wolf has good nighttime vision, so it can hunt when the light is fading at dusk and even in the darkest dead of night.

HEARING

The wolf has large ears and a very acute sense of hearing. A wolf can hear high-pitched sounds that we cannot hear, and it can pick up sounds that are a long distance away. A wolf can hear about 6 miles (9.5 km) away in a forest, and about 10 miles (16 km) away in open areas, where the sound carries better.

The wolf's eyes are placed on the front of its head, so it can focus on prey that lies in front.

A wolf needs to be alert at all times in case of danger. When a wolf is sleeping, its ears will be in an upright position, so it can catch any sounds made by other animals. A wolf can use each ear on its own, turning the ear to locate where a noise is coming from.

SMELL

The wolf has an amazing sense of smell, which is considered to be about one hundred times better than the sense of smell of humans. The wolf uses its sense of smell to track prey. A wolf pack has been reported scenting a moose cow with twin calves at a distance of four miles (6.5 km). A wolf can still smell an animal three days after it has left an area.

The wolf also uses its sense of smell to find out if wolves from neighboring packs have come visiting its territory. A wolf has two scent glands at the base of its tail. The glands produce a scented discharge, which is different in every wolf. This individual scent means that

The wolf uses its nose to discover all the important information, such as which wolves have come visiting and the whereabouts of prey.

the urine or droppings a wolf uses to mark its territory will carry the wolf's personal identification.

TASTE

Wolves can taste different flavors, such as bitter, sweet, and salty.

Discovering Special skills

The wolf is an expert hunter because of the special skills it has developed to plan a hunt, find a **victim**, such as one that is sick and ailing, and stage an **ambush**.

PLANNING

The first task for a wolf pack is to find prey to hunt. This is where the wolf's extraordinary sense of smell is called upon. The wolves pick up the scent of an animal, such as a deer or a bison, and follow the scent trail until they find the herd. When a herd is faced with an enemy, the animals close ranks. The biggest adults face outward, surrounding and protecting the calves. The herd cannot stay like this forever. It has to break up to feed. This is the moment when the wolves chase individual animals.

SELECTING A VICTIM

Herd animals take flight at the first sign of trouble, and fast-moving

Wolves meet and spend some time together before setting off on a hunt.

When prey is spotted, the wolves step up their pace as they prepare to attack.

prey, such as deer and pronghorn, can outrun a pack of wolves. If the wolves are not successful at their first attempt, they will not give up. A wolf pack will pursue a herd for days at a time, following the animals' scent tracks if the herd goes out of sight. The wolves study the herd, looking for calves or sick animals that are struggling to keep up with the rest of the herd. The wolves will then focus on one of these animals, running at it and snapping at its heels.

TEAM WORK

The wolf pack is now ready to chase its chosen victim. The victim animal starts to run, but, over a short distance, the wolves will be able to outrun a weak animal.

The wolves work as a team to surround their victim so that it cannot escape. When the prey animal falls to the ground, the wolves spring onto its underbelly and bite to try to kill it.

The claws of a wolf are not sharp enough to grip prey. Instead of using their claws, the wolves use their teeth to bite into the animal, hanging onto the victim's body as the victim struggles to get free of the wolves.

In spite of the wolf pack's extremely efficient teamwork, only about 30 percent of their hunts will be successful.

13

What Does a Wolf Do All Day?

A wolf pack is a tight-knit group that keeps itself well hidden. To find out the secrets of how wolves spend their time, scientists go into wilderness areas to study them, while they take care to stay hidden themselves.

AT THE DEN
In the spring and summer, a wolf pack finds a home base in its territory so that cubs can be reared. This home may be a cave, or the wolves may dig a den. The pack spends most of the day at the den site. A wolf dozes rather than going into a deep sleep because it needs to be alert for danger.

GROOMING
The wolf relies on its thick coat in the cold winter months and will spend much of its leisure time licking through its own hair, keeping its coat in good order. If a wolf is very muddy, it may take a bath in a river or a pond.

Wolves in a pack also groom each other. This kind of grooming is a wolf's way of making close ties with others and sorting out positions within the pack. Wolves consider it a great honor to groom

When a wolf is resting, it stays on the alert, listening for possible danger.

A high-ranking wolf patrols the boundaries of the pack's territory, using its nose to find out if wolves from neighboring packs have come visiting.

the top-ranking male or female. Wolves will often comfort a sick wolf by grooming it.

PLAYING

Adult wolves play with each other, staging mock fights and chasing each other. This play is another way of forming close links with all members of the pack.

ON PATROL

A wolf pack needs to guard its territory. The higher-ranking wolves in the pack are needed for this job. They leave scent messages around their territory that tell other wolves to keep out.

HUNTING

The best time for hunting is when the light is fading. When cubs are in the pack, one adult remains behind to babysit, and the rest of the pack sets off in the early evening. They will not return until the next morning. If a hunt is successful, the wolves feast on the carcass. An adult can eat about 33 pounds (15 kg) of meat at one sitting. Sometimes a wolf pack remains near a kill for several days, until they have eaten the whole carcass.

TRAVELING

Wolves are great travelers and spend much of their time on the move in the fall and in the winter. Wolves travel in single file with the pack leader at the front. They take routes alongside lakes, rivers, and streams where they are likely to find prey animals grazing. When traveling, the wolves rest wherever they find shelter.

How Do Wolves Communicate?

The wolves in a pack must understand each other so that they can hunt as a team and bond as a family group. By watching wolves in the wild, scientists have learned many of the ways in which wolves communicate with one another. They have also learned what information wolves share.

MEETING AND GREETING

When pack members meet each other, they do not just say "hello." They use their bodies to show one another which wolf has a higher ranking in the pack.

The highest-ranking male or female stands tall, with its head held high and its tail slightly lifted.

A low-ranking wolf (*right*) meets the pack leader and shows respect for the leader by lowering its head.

When a low-ranking wolf meets a high-ranking wolf, it shows its respect by flattening its ears, keeping its body position low, and its tail between its legs. The low-ranking wolf may even roll onto its back.

The cubs in a pack lick the adults' lips as a form of greeting. In fact, they are asking the adults to **regurgitate** food for them after a hunt. A low-ranking adult wolf may lick the lips of a high-ranking wolf to say "I am as harmless as a cub. Please look after me." A friendly adult will respond by flattening its ears slightly and wagging its tail.

KEEPING ORDER

Sometimes a low-ranking wolf tries to improve its position in the pack by challenging a wolf of a higher rank. The challenging wolf stands at full height. It may raise the hair along its back so that it looks even bigger and more ferocious. The wolf holds its tail high and may curl back its lip. If the higher-ranking wolf accepts the challenge, the two may fight.

The pack leader works hard to keep order and settle disputes. In most cases, after much growling and snarling, the weaker wolf gives up and slinks away in defeat.

When a hunt is successful, the top-ranking wolves eat first, and will drive away lower-ranking members of the pack with growls and snarls.

After a successful hunt, the top-ranking male and female always eat first. They growl fiercely at lower-ranking wolves, making them wait their turn.

WOLF SOUNDS

Wolves communicate with each by using different sounds that are like a special wolf language. They speak with growls, snarls, whines, yelps, whimpers, barks, and howls.

A wolf will bark as a warning, alerting other members of the pack to danger.

GROWLS AND SNARLS

Growls and snarls are used as signs of **aggression**. A growl is a low, rumbling sound, which is a warning, usually given by a high-ranking wolf. It means "Watch out or you will be in trouble." A mother wolf may growl at a cub if it is getting too boisterous, which is her way of telling the cub to settle down and mind its manners. If a wolf snarls, with its lips curled back, it is likely to attack.

BARKS

A wolf does not bark very often. If a wolf sees or hears something out of the ordinary that could be a danger, it gives a sharp bark to warn other member of the pack.

WHINES AND WHIMPERS

Young wolf cubs whimper when they are hungry or cold. A wolf may also whine when it is in pain.

Sometimes a wolf returning to the pack may be greeted with low, welcoming whines from other members of the pack.

YELPS

A yelp is a sharp cry of pain and is usually heard when a wolf has been nipped by another wolf.

HOWLING

The wolf is famous for howling, and people have often been frightened by this strange cry when it echoes through the night. Wolf howls sound especially frightening because all the members of the pack howl together. Wolves howl for a number of reasons:

- To bring a pack together so they can set off on a journey.
- To build group spirit, especially when they gather and howl together before going on a hunt.
- To claim ownership of territory, warning other wolf packs to keep away.
- To reunite pack members after a hunt.

The highest-ranking male and female start the howling and are quickly joined by other members of the pack. The sound can be heard from a distance of 10 miles (16 km).

SCENT MESSAGES

Wolves also communicate with each other by leaving scent messages. When a wolf pack is on the **boundary** of its territory, scent marking increases dramatically. As well as leaving scent messages in urine and droppings, a wolf may scratch trees or paw the ground. This action releases an odor from a gland in its paw, which can be smelled by other wolves.

The sound of howling wolves fills the night air and can be heard for many miles.

Times of Trouble

A wolf living in a pack has few enemies to fear, because the pack is powerful enough to kill or chase away all large meat-eating hunters. Brown bears have been known to kill wolf cubs, but there are also reports of wolves driving away cougars and even bears that come too close to a wolf den site. The teamwork of the wolf pack allows it to drive off larger animals.

RIVAL PACKS

The greatest danger that a wolf pack faces is when a fight breaks out with a neighboring wolf pack. Wolves try to prevent this from happening by scent-marking along the boundaries of their territory, warning wolves from nearby packs to keep away.

At times, however, two packs meet, and the results are often

If a wolf is threatened by a bigger, stronger wolf, it will submit to avoid a fight.

A fight between two healthy males will not end until one of the wolves is killed, driven off, or is badly injured and accepts defeat.

disastrous. The top-ranking rival males will start a fight. Both animals are usually fit and strong, and, in most cases, they will fight until one of the wolves is dead.

If a wolf is injured during a fight, it faces grave danger because the wound may become infected and the wolf will struggle to keep up with the rest of the pack. Pack members do not desert a sick wolf. Wolves have been seen grooming an injured wolf, giving comfort and helping to clean its wounds.

FIGHTS WITHIN THE PACK

The top-ranking wolf maintains order and discipline within the pack, but the pack does have times of conflict. Conflicts may occur in the breeding season if a lower-ranking male tries to breed with the top-ranking female. More often, fights happen if the top-ranking wolf is old and losing its powers. A young wolf will challenge the leader, and the fight only ends when one wolf is killed or is driven away.

OLD AGE

Life in the wild is very tough as a wolf battles to find food, to steer clear of fights, and to live through intensely cold winters. Most wolves only survive in the wild until they are between seven and eight years old.

In a zoo, a wolf may live for fifteen years or more, because it is provided with food and has no real dangers to face.

When Wolves Are Ready to Breed

For some animals living in the wild, the breeding season is primarily a time to search for a partner. In a wolf pack, the opposite is true. Adult males and females live together all year long, so when breeding season comes, they are available for one another. The pack, however, has strict rules that limit which animals can breed.

RULE OF THE PACK
A wolf pack consists of a top-ranking male and female, older cubs, and a number of other related wolves. It is only the top-ranking male and female who produce a litter of cubs. When the top-ranking female in the pack is ready for breeding, between January and March, she

The top-ranking male and female will be the only wolves in the pack that will breed.

only accepts the top-ranking male. This wolf, which is the biggest and strongest in the pack, will fend off the challenges of younger males. He also stops other pack members from breeding with each other. This control may cause trouble in the pack, but in most cases, the lower-ranking males give in to the leader. The top-ranking male and female breed together each year and are often partners for life.

SURVIVAL OF THE FITTEST

The leader is the most fit wolf, so the leader is accepted as the one that will breed the strongest cubs. Why does the pack leader prevent other litters from being born in the pack? This practice is a matter of survival. The pack's main concern is to get enough food for all the members. If only one litter of cubs is produced each year, the pack has a good chance of finding enough food to feed the cubs, and the cubs will then have the best chance of surviving.

PREPARATIONS

When wolves are traveling, they are not fussy about where they stop to rest. All they need is a leafy bed at the foot of a tree or a scraped spot in the earth or snow. When a female is expecting cubs, however, she needs to find a place of safety. The female finds a cave, or she may take over a burrow that has been abandoned by another animal. The **pregnant** wolf will then start digging to create a den. Most dens have a number of entrances and a long tunnel, about 20 feet (6 m) long, that leads to the burrow where the cubs will be born.

Wolves form close relationships, and a male and female may be partners for life, raising a litter of cubs every year.

The Family Life of Wolves

A female wolf is pregnant for nine weeks. Then she retreats to her underground den and gives birth to her cubs in secrecy. Her average litter size is six cubs.

NEWBORN CUBS

When the cubs are born, they are blind and helpless. All they can do is squirm toward their mother to drink her milk, but they develop quickly. Within two weeks, their eyes are open, and they are up on their feet. During this time, the rest of the pack does not travel. It stays at the den site and brings back food for the mother so that she can stay with her cubs.

When the cubs are three to four weeks old, the mother encourages them to come out of the den, where they will meet the other members of the pack. The older wolves greet the cubs with soft whimpers of welcome and much tail-wagging. From this moment, all the members of the pack help look after the cubs.

THE BABYSITTER

When the cubs are six to eight weeks old, they no longer take milk from their mother. The cubs

The mother wolf cares for her cubs, feeding them and protecting them.

The wolf cubs must stay at the den site while their mother goes hunting.

rely on members of the pack to bring food to them. The pack goes on a hunt, leaving one adult who acts as a babysitter to the cubs. The cubs are happy to play outside the den, but playing outside can be dangerous. Bears and golden eagles can attack wolf cubs.

When the pack returns from a hunt, the cubs run up to the adults, wagging their tails and whining. The cubs lick the faces of the adults. This licking is a signal for the adults to regurgitate partly digested food for the cubs to eat. Licking is also a way of forming close links between the adult and the cubs, so they become a close-knit family group.

PLAYTIME

Wolf cubs are very playful and spend much of their time chasing each other, wrestling, tumbling, and having mock fights. The cubs are not just having fun. They are learning how to use their bodies and getting ready for the time when they will go hunting. Adults also play with the cubs. An adult will let a cub crawl all over it and have play-biting sessions. In this way, the adult wolf teaches the cub how to fight. If the cub's play becomes too out of control, the adult will give a warning growl. The cubs need to learn to obey the higher-ranking members of the pack from an early age.

The Wolf Cubs Grow Up

In the summer months, while the cubs are growing up, the pack gives up its traveling way of life to help care for the new members of the pack.

A NEW SCHOOL

When the cubs are about eight weeks of age, the pack moves from the den site to a new base, which is known as the **rendezvous site**. This site is where the cubs start to learn more about hunting. When the pack meets to set off for a hunt, the cubs howl with the other wolves, but they are not allowed to go on the hunt. The cubs must stay behind under the watchful eye of a babysitter. The cubs practice their hunting skills, chasing rodents

Young wolves run and play together, which helps them perfect the hunting skills they will need when they become adults.

A wolf faces a tough future if it leaves the safety of the pack.

and catching bugs. The adults return from the hunt with bones and other parts of the carcass so the cubs learn how to feed themselves.

MOVING ON
By the time the cubs are six months old, the pack begins traveling again. This time is hard for cubs. They must keep up with the adults and must also start to help with the hunts. Many cubs die during their first winter.

GOING SOLO
The cubs stay with the pack for the winter months. Then it is decision time. Some young adults stay with their family pack all their lives. A wolf may move up the ranking positions in a pack as it gets older, and it may even take over as leader of the pack.

If food is scarce, however, a young wolf may decide to leave the pack and go it alone. This is a difficult decision for a wolf. A lone wolf must survive without the support of the pack and it is forced to live on a poor diet of small animals, because it cannot hunt large prey on its own. A single wolf will lead a **solitary** life, keeping out of the way of other wolf packs.

In the breeding season, the lone wolf will go in search of a partner. If the wolf is successful, and a litter of cubs is produced, the months of struggling alone will have paid off. The lone wolf will be the leader of the new wolf pack it has created.

Wolves and People

The wolf has been a very successful animal in the wild, but it is now in real danger of becoming **extinct**. Wolves are now found in only 3 percent of the land they once occupied throughout North America.

FEAR OF THE WOLF

From earliest civilizations, people have been frightened of wolves. Myths and legends have spread that show the wolf as a creature of evil, and there have been reports of wolves attacking people. In fact, wolves usually try to keep away from people. A wolf pack's main crime has been hunting cattle and other livestock. People have been so determined to wipe out the wolf that they have not tried to balance their needs with that of the wolf.

The wolf has been hated and feared, and in North America, an attempt to kill all free-roaming wolves was nearly successful.

Wilderness areas where wolves can live and breed are fast disappearing.

The population of wolves throughout the world has fallen. In North America, the wolf has suffered dramatically. European settlers brought their hatred of wolves to the new continent. From the 1860s onward, many people were determined to get rid of all living wolves by trapping, poisoning, and shooting them. Many cattle ranchers had packs of dogs they used to keep wolves away from their herds. From the late 1800s through the 1920s, the U.S. government and many states paid a **bounty** for every wolf killed.

A BRIGHTER FUTURE?

It was not until the 1970s that people started to understand the the wolf and to value this great animal. They began to balance the needs of cattle ranchers against the needs of wolves. By this time, so few wolves were left in the wild that they were in danger of dying out forever. Killing wolves was outlawed, but the wolf was faced with another threat. A wolf pack can only do well if it has a large territory with a good number of prey animals. Today, **wilderness** areas are fast disappearing and the wolf is in grave danger of having no where to live. Projects have been funded to reintroduce wolves to areas where they once lived in great numbers. Because of these efforts, Yellowstone National Park and other wildlife **refuge** areas in North America now have wolf populations again. Wolves are now protected by law, and conservation groups help support their refuges.

Glossary

adaptable able to change or adjust to new conditions

aggression threatening behavior

ambush a surprise attack

boundary the dividing line that separates two territories

bounty a reward of money

camouflage appearance colored and marked so that it hides or blends in with the surroundings

canines the biting teeth

carcass the body of a dead animal

endurance the ability to keep active over a long period of time

extinct having died out completely as a species

mammal a warm-blooded animal that is covered with fur, gives birth to live young, and produces milk

marrow fatty or blood cell-producing tissues found in the centers of bones

pack leader the top male or female who makes all the decisions for a wolf pack

predator a hunter that kills other animals for food

pregnant carrying an unborn baby inside the female's body until it is time to give birth

prey animals animals chosen as food by meat-eating hunters

refuge a wilderness area that is set aside as a protected home for an endangered group of animals

regurgitate to bring up partly digested food for cubs to eat

rendezvous site a place where the pack meets after a hunting trip, and where the pups wait with a babysitter until the adults return

solitary an animal that lives and hunts alone

territory the land occupied by a wolf pack or other animals, which they defend from others, including competitors of their own species

top-ranking an animal that is rated in the top position in its pack or group

victim a prey animal chosen by a meat-eating hunter

wilderness a wild place where no people live or work and where animals live by their own means

More Books to Read

Little Wolves. Born to be Wild (series). Helene Montarde
  (Gareth Stevens Publishing)

Once a Wolf: How Wildlife Biologists Fought to Bring Back the Gray Wolf.
  Stephen R. Swinburne (Houghton Mifflin)

The Life Cycle of a Wolf. The Life Cycle (series). Bobbie Kalman (Crabtree
  Publishing Company)

Wolves. Our Wild World (series). Laura Evert (Northword Press)

Wolves. William John Ripple (Pebble Books)

Web Sites

Boomer Wolf Site
www.boomerwolf.com/

Gray Wolves
www.thewildones.org/Animals/grayWolf.html

Kids Rendezvous site: Information on Wolves
www.timberwolfinformation.org/kidsonly/kidsinfo.htm

World Almanac Wolves
www.worldalmanacforkids.com/explore/animals/wolf.html

Publishers note to educators and parents: Our editors have carefully reviewed these
Web sites to ensure that they are suitable for children. Many Web sites change frequently,
however, and we cannot guarantee that a site's future contents will continue to meet our
high standards of quality and educational value. Be advised that children should be closely
supervised whenever they access the Internet.

Index